Party Cakes

James Winterflood

Φ CONTINENTAL PUBLICATIONS, Ltd.

Introduction

Having a party is one of the nicest ways of getting together with your friends and is very much appreciated by children and adults alike. A party conjures up thoughts of good companions, happiness and that extra special treat, provided by the host but also, very often, by those attending the occasion.

The reasons for having a party vary considerably but one thing which is always prominent is the party cake or centerpiece. So many hosts have longed to provide just the right cake for the occasion but unfortunately have not been able to do so. This may be because they lack expertise, or maybe they are unable to combine the right association of ideas with the subject of the party.

It is hoped that this book will enable you to both increase your decorating skill and help you to devise the exact type of party cake you wish to have, any time the need should arise.

Whether making cakes or just reading about them, may you have lasting enjoyment from **Party Cakes.**

James Winterflood

Contents

Published by Continental Publications, Ltd., P.O. Box 1729, Carlsbad California.

Awknowledgements:
Photography by F. H. Stapleton — Studio Frankfurt, London, England
Cake Bases by C.S. Worth, Welling, Kent, England
Marzipan by John F. Renshaw & Co. Ltd., Mitcham, Surrey, England
Editing by Mary Darveau and Jane Johnson, Torrance California
Graphics/Production by Christina Doussa-Burton, Palos Verdes, California

Making Party Cakes

CAKE BASES

Choosing the right type of cake base for the party cake will ensure easy handling and a satisfying result. For example, a soft delicate sponge would not be a good choice for a cake that must stand on its side or must carry additional weight (the clock or the well).

Although most of the cakes illustrated are of the genoese or sponge type, fruit cake and other types can be used, especially when the cake is for an adult party. Since fruit cake is used in a block, joining is not necessary. Adhesion of the covering or masking material onto fruit cake should be made with a good jam puree, not buttercream.

CAKE SHAPES

Many of the cakes illustrated in this book are not of the traditional shape and, unless shaped tins can be purchased, they are best cut to shape from a baked sheet or block of cake. There is a set of templates available for this purpose.

The cake trimmings left over when cutting shapes in this way need not be wasted. They can form a perfect base for a trifle, and an alternative use is given in the recipes at the end of the book.

MARZIPAN AND SUGAR PASTE

Either marzipan or sugar paste are ideal to use when making party cakes, but other mediums such as fondant, fudges, chocolate, buttercream and soft icings can be used where desired.

Marzipan and sugar paste are best kept in a plastic bag to prevent crusting caused by exposure to the air. If this should occur and the crust is thick, cut it away before using. The wrapped pastes can be stored in a cool, well ventilated cupboard or in a plastic box with a tight-fitting lid. Never store in a humid or dusty atmosphere.

Both pastes are easily colored by using either paste or liquid vegetable colors. Never use weak colors; too much must be added to attain the desired effect and this makes the pastes soft and sticky. Flavors may be added as desired.

When rolling the pastes to the required thickness, always be sure that they are free to move on the rolling surface by dusting it with icing or powdered sugar. After dusting, rub the surface with the hand to dry it before applying the rolling pin or spotting will occur, especially on colored pastes.

The greatest problems in connection with marzipan and sugar paste are flour dust and yeast spores, both of which cause the pastes to ferment and render them useless. Be extremely careful not to use flour or yeast in the same area that marzipan or sugar paste is being worked. All surfaces should be thoroughly washed before rolling out pastes on them.

Hands and fingernails should be well scrubbed to ensure absolute cleanliness and the hands well dried so that no excessive moisture is transmitted to the pastes. Excessive moisture will make the pastes sticky and unmanageable, and if they are stored this way it will create a perfect medium for mold growth.

ROLLING PINS

As most people find it difficult to use icings or to carry out complicated piping exercises, the cakes in this book have been carefully designed to be decorated by rolling out paste coverings.

To enhance the appearance of the pastes, two types of patterned rolling pins have been used. Both can be easily made from wooden dowel and electrical cable.

Single strand rolling pin

Items needed:
  1 piece of wooden dowel or rod,
    18" long and 1¼" in diameter
  75' of plastic covered electrical bell wire
    ¹⁄₁₆" thick
  2 small nails

Nail one end of the wire to the dowel approximately 3" in from one end. Wind the wire tightly around the dowel so that each coil touches the preceeding one and continue until the wire is used up. This will give a covered section of about 12" in length, leaving a 3" handle at each end. Secure the end of the wire with the second nail.

Twin strand rolling pin

Items needed:
  1 piece of wooden dowel or rod
    18" long and 1¼" in diameter
  42' of plastic covered electrical wire ⅛"
    thick or 20' of pre-twisted electrical wire
  2 small nails

Fold the wire in half, making two strands 21' long, and twist them together along their entire length. This will give a twisted length of 20'. Nail one end of the wire 3" in from the end of the dowel and wind the wire tightly around the dowel do that each coil is as close as possible to the preceeding one. Because of its twisting nature there will be gaps between each coil. When all the wire is used up, secure the other end with the second nail. This will give a covered section of about 12" in length.

These plastic-covered pins will leave a good imprint in the marzipan or sugar paste without sticking. They can be easily washed or brushed with a stiff nail brush to clean. Never soak the rolling pins in water and dry immediately after washing.

MAKING YOUR PARTY CAKE A SUCCESS

Before attempting to produce any cake in this book, be sure to read the instructions thoroughly and have all necessary materials and tools at hand. Keep a damp cloth handy and lightly dampen scissors, knives and cutters before cutting marzipan or sugar paste. This will produce a good clean edge for a superior finish.

It may be helpful to practice on dummy blocks (wood or polystyrene) until the degree of skill required can be satisfactorily transfered to the party cake.

Finally, please remember that not everyone can be an expert but with practice, a lot of people can be very good.

Drum

Split two 8" x 1¼" sponges, one white and one chocolate, into 8" x ¾" rounds, making four rounds in all. Join the rounds with chocolate buttercream, alternating colors.

Roll out a strip of yellow marzipan or sugar paste ⅛" thick and of sufficient length to encircle the side of the cake. (26" long for an 8" diameter cake.) Roll it wide enough to cover the depth of the cake and mark it in a diamond pattern with a single strand rolling pin. Trim to the size required. Starting at one end, roll up like a catherine wheel, the markings being rolled inside.

Mask the side of the cake with a little buttercream and stand the cake on a flat working surface. Place the plain surface flap of the rolled marzipan up to it and slowly unroll the marzipan around the side. This will cover the side, leaving the marked surface showing. Press all around the cake with the palms of the hands to ensure adhesion.

Make the skin of the drum by rolling out white marzipan or sugar paste ⅛" thick and large enough to cover the top of the cake. Turn the marzipan over onto a piece of waxed paper and after coating the top of the cake with a little buttercream, turn the cake upside down onto the marzipan. Using a sharp pointed knife, cut carefully around the edge of the

cake to remove the surplus marzipan and turn the cake back onto its base. The drum skin will now be in place.

The top and bottom rims are made by rolling out red marzipan or sugar paste ⅛" thick. Cut two strips 1" x 26" and roll up as described for the side. Stick these to the side of the drum, using a little egg white, water or melted chocolate. Roll out six strings of white marzipan or sugar paste 7" long and ¼" diameter. Fold each string in half and twist to form a rope. Trim to size and after drying thoroughly, stick into place around the side of the drum.

Use lollipops for the drum sticks, and lengthen the handles by inserting them into drinking straws cut to the size required. Any inscription should be placed on the skin of the drum before the drumsticks are added.

Quantities used:
Marzipan or sugar paste

Drum side	8 ozs
Drum top	3 ozs
2 rims	6 ozs
6 ropes	3 ozs
Buttercream	14 ozs

Bowl of Tulips

Trim the bottom of an 8" diameter fruit cake 1" up from the bottom and 1" in from the side. The cake will taper to a 6" base. Brush or spread a very thin coating of apricot jam onto the top of the cake and dress with a mixture of light and dark chocolate vermicelli to form the earth.

Roll out pink marzipan or sugar paste ⅛" thick to measure 26" long and of sufficient width to cover the side of the cake, plus ½" extra to turn down on the top. Mark with twin strand rolling pin in a lengthwise fashion and trim to size. Turn the marzipan over onto a clean piece of waxed paper and spread a very thin coat of jam onto the back. Roll the cake up inside the marzipan leaving a ½" overlap at the top.

Stand the cake back on its base and gently press in the bottom edge to the tapered side. Turn the top flap down onto the top of the cake to overlap the chocolate vermicelli.

Roll out two strings of pink marzipan or sugar paste 24" long and ¼" diameter and twist them to form a rope. Slightly dampen the turned down rim on top of the cake and place the rope on it.

Roll out green marzipan or sugar paste ⅛" thick for the bulbs and cut ten leaves ¾" x 2¼", tapered to a point at both ends. From the surplus make five cone-shaped pieces for the bulb centers. Flatten the leaves at the edges; for each bulb wrap two leaves around a cone, overlapping at the edges; pull the tips outward and slightly downward.

Trim the bottoms of the bulbs flat and stand upright on the cake. Add the inscription either directly onto the cake top or pipe onto a ribbon of marzipan before placing into position.

Quantities used:

Marzipan or sugar paste

Side	12 ozs
2 strings (for rope)	1¾ ozs each
Bulbs (complete)	½ oz each
Vermicelli	1½ ozs
Jam	1 oz

6

Clock

Split and join with buttercream a 10" x 2½" round cake or use two genoese cake discs each 10" x 1¼". For eye appeal two different colors are ideal. From one side measure in 1¼" and cut in a straight line across the cake, removing the small curved section; reserve it.*

Roll out pink marzipan or sugar paste to a ⅛" thickness and mark the surface with a single strand rolling pin in a squared pattern. Turn the marzipan over onto waxed paper and after masking the top of the cake with a little buttercream, turn the cake over on to it. With a sharp knife trim around the cake to remove the surplus marzipan.

Mask the side of the cake with buttercream but do not mask the flat edge where the curved piece has been cut away. Dress the side with chocolate vermicelli.

Cut out the numbers from marzipan or sugar paste and stick them into place or pipe them directly onto the cake using colored icing or buttercream.

Roll out red, chocolate and white marzipan to ⅛" thicknesses. The eyes are made of 1⅝" white discs and 1" chocolate discs, the nose is made of a 1" disc and the mouth is a crescent cut from a 3" disc. Make the hands of the clock as shown in the illustration. The hands should be placed in such a way as to denote the age of the recipient. Place the eyes, nose and mouth on the cake.

Make the feet by cutting the top ½" away from the small curved section previously removed from the cake and then cut in two across the middle as illustrated. Mask with buttercream and dress with chocolate vermicelli. Stand them side by side and after piping a small bulb of buttercream onto each one place the cake firmly onto them. Add a party hat for decoration. Any inscription required should be placed on the cake board or the side of the cake.

*Should a cake be required which is laying flat, do not cut out this section for the feet; leave the cake completely round.

Note: The back of the cake can be coated with chocolate or masked with buttercream and dressed with vermicelli to seal it.

Quantities used:

Marzipan or sugar paste

Face	7 ozs
Mouth	½ oz
Nose	¼ oz
Eyes (white)	½ oz for 2
Eyes (chocolate)	¼ oz for 2
Hands	¼ oz for 2
Numbers	?? oz
Buttercream	1 lb
Vermicelli (side and feet only)	2 ozs

Fish

Cut two pieces of sponge or genoese cake, 12" x 7" x 1¼", into an oval shape as shown and join with buttercream. Coat the cake completely with buttercream. Dress the sides with roasted chopped nuts, including a half-inch border on the top of the cake.

Roll brown marzipan or sugar paste ¼" thick and cut the tail, dorsal and anal fins. Make the tail 4" at its narrow end, 6" at the wide end and 2½" across. Mark the tail with the prongs of a table fork. Cut in a 'V' shape from the tips of the 6" line to the middle, 1" in, as shown. Make the anal fin from a triangle 2½" x 2½" x 1¾" and mark with a fork. Make the dorsal fin by cutting a wedge shape 2" x 3" and mark with fork with the lines running up and down. Make the other two fins from rolled oval marzipan or paste pieces, flattened with the hand and marked with a fork. Make the pectoral fin 2¾" long and the ventral fin 1½" long. Allow all the fins to dry or coat the backs with chocolate to make them rigid.

Roll yellow marzipan or paste ¹⁄₁₆" thick and cut 18 1¾" diameter discs and 13 1½" diameter discs for the scales.

Make the head by rolling yellow paste ⅛" thick. Cut a 4¼" diameter disc and trim one side to fit the front of the cake.

Fix the tail and the dorsal and anal fins onto the cake with the edges just touching the creamed surface. Position the scales starting with two lines at the tail, using some of the smaller discs. Overlap each line and use the larger discs as the cake widens. Fill in the edges and around the head with the rest of the small discs. Place the head on last.

Make the eyes from two ⅛" discs, one white, 1½" diameter, and the other brown, 1" diameter. Place as shown. Make the mouth from a stick of red marzipan or paste 3½" x ½". Fold in half and roll one end to a sharp point, curve downward and position on the head. Place the pectoral and ventral fins as shown.

Quantities used:

Marzipan or sugar paste	
Tail	1½ ozs
Dorsal, anal fins	¼ oz each
Pectoral fin	½ oz
Ventral fin	¼ oz
Head	1¾ oz
Scales	5½ ozs
Eye (white)	¼ oz
Eye (brown)	⅛ oz
Mouth	½ oz
Buttercream	1 lb
Nuts	2½ ozs

Bowling Alley

Join with coffee buttercream two genoese or sponge cakes 12" x 7" x 1¼". Roll out brown marzipan or sugar paste to ⅛" thick and mark with a single strand rolling pin along its length.

Cut down one side with a sharp knife following the line of the marking rolling pin. This will give a straight side in line with the marks you have made. Turn the marzipan over onto a piece of waxed paper and after coating the top of the cake with a little buttercream, turn the cake over onto the marzipan, keeping the side of the cake in line with the straight edge of the marzipan. Trim the marzipan to fit the cake. Turn the cake back onto its base and you should now have the marzipan or sugar paste top in position with the lines running lengthwise.

Mask the sides with a little buttercream and dress them with a mixture of chocolate vermicelli and green chopped nuts or green sugar strands.

Using yellow marzipan or sugar paste, cut a bar to the shape illustrated, making sure it is long enough to fit the length of the cake (12") and ½" wide. Use a piece of wooden dowel or the handle of a wooden spoon to mark the indent along its length and fix into place.

Make twenty bowling pins using white marzipan or sugar paste. Follow carefully the stages shown. The pins should be 1¾" in height. When they are dry fix them into place. The balls used are either round sweets (candies) or chocolate covered honeycomb centers but any round candy will do.

Add the inscription and place onto a board decorated as shown.

Quantities used:

Marzipan or sugar paste

Top	8 ozs
Bar	2 ozs
Pins	¼ oz each
Buttercream	1 lb
Dressing	2¼ ozs

Party Cracker

Spread a 10" x 12" x ½" sponge cake with flavored buttercream; beginning with a short side, roll as you would a jelly roll. If the skin is loose either remove it or roll the sponge so that the skin is inside. Spread a little buttercream on both ends and dip them into roasted, chopped or flaked almonds.

Roll colored marzipan or sugar paste ⅛" thick; cut a rectangle 11" wide and of sufficient length to completely cover the circumference of the roll. Use a knife to cut the top and bottom edges, but cut the sides with a fluted pastry wheel to make them crinkled.

Turn marzipan onto a sheet of waxed paper and spread a thin layer of buttercream on it, leaving a 1" margin unfrosted on each side. Place the sponge roll onto the top edge and roll up in the marzipan, using gentle pressure to ensure good adhesion.

To mark the cracker use a ⅜"-diameter wooden or plastic rod. Place the rod 3" from the end of the roll and rock backwards and forwards, pressing down into the marzipan until a deep ring is formed. Repeat on the other end.

Decorate with sugar leaves and flowers; add a small plaque bearing a special inscription. Or spin a design on top with melted chocolate, using a spiral motion, then decorate.

Quantities used:

Marzipan or sugar paste	14 ozs
Nuts	½ oz
Buttercream	10 ozs

14

Snakes and Ladders

Join with lemon buttercream two 9" x 9" x 1¼" squares of cake, one pink and one chocolate. Spread a thin layer of buttercream on the top surface of the cake.

Roll out orange marzipan or sugar paste ⅛" thick to cover an area 9" x 9". Turn the marzipan over onto a clean piece of waxed paper; turn the cake over onto it so that the creamed surface sticks to the marzipan. With a sharp knife trim the marzipan.

Mark the squares on top of the cake with the back of a long knife or the edge of a ruler. Measure ½" in from the edge of the cake and make the first line by pressing down into the marzipan with the marker. Now measure off at 1" intervals across the cake and mark in the lines, finishing with another ½" border. Turn the cake and repeat to form the squares. You should have 64 squares with a ½" border.

Roll out brown marzipan or sugar paste ⅛" thick and mark it in a criss-cross fashion with a single strand rolling pin. Cut four strips ½" wide and 10" long. Dampen the ½" borders of the cake and lay the strips onto them, overlapping the corners as illustrated. Cut down through the overlaps diagonally with a sharp knife to form a mitred join. Remove the surplus marzipan to complete the border.

Mask the sides of the cake with buttercream and dress with a mixture of dark chocolate vermicelli and green chopped nuts.

Use green marzipan or sugar paste for the snakes and make as shown. The ladders are piped out with chocolate onto a piece of waxed paper to the desired length.

Complete the cake by putting on the required inscription and arranging the snakes and ladders around it. Add small sugar flowers for counters.

Quantities used:

Marzipan or sugar paste	
Cake top	8 ozs
4 border strips	1½ ozs
Snakes	¼ oz each
Buttercream	14 ozs
Dressing	2 ozs

Money Bag

Bake two sponges in 6" diameter bread pans. The pans should have sloping sides to give a base measurement of 5" diameter.

Join the two sponges with coffee or chocolate buttercream, the two larger faces to the center. Spread a little cream on one of the smaller outside faces and dip into roasted flaked or sliced almonds.

Roll out brown marzipan or sugar paste ⅛" thick. Cut out a 15" diameter circle. Turn the disc over onto a clean working surface and spread a little cream in the center.

Turn the sponge over onto its nutted surface. Holding it to the table with the palm of the hand, spread a little cream around the side, taking care not to get any cream on the table surface. Pick up the marzipan disc and, working from the back, drop it over the sponge so that the cream on the disc engages with the bottom of the sponge. Allow the marzipan to fall naturally down the sides and arrange

the folds around the sponge, pressing gently with the palms of the hands to ensure adhesion. Turn the cake onto its base.

Roll out a string of marzipan or sugar paste 6" long and tie to form a loose knot. Cut through the loop. Making two holes in the edge of the cake just below the rim, insert the two ends.

Add "chocolate gold coins" to complete the money bag. Mount the cake on a board and if an inscription is needed put it on the board around the cake.

Quantities used:
Marzipan or sugar paste

For the disc	12 ozs
For the string	½ oz
Buttercream	6 ozs
Roasted almonds	1 oz

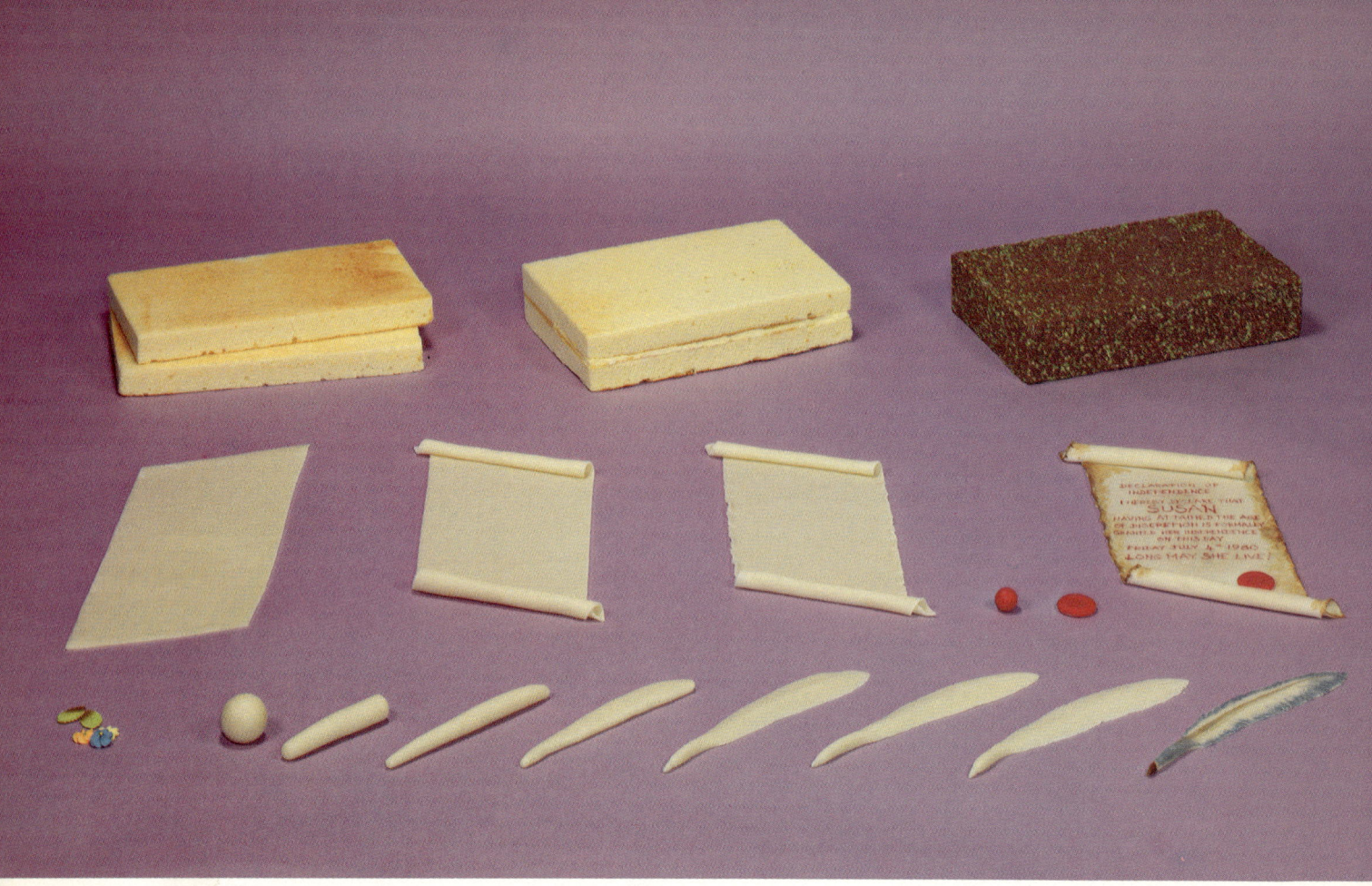

Scroll

Join with buttercream two pieces of sponge or genoese cake 12" x 7" x 1¼". Mask the top and sides with buttercream and dress with a mixture of chocolate vermicelli and green chopped nuts.

To make the scroll, roll out a piece of white marzipan or sugar paste to a 1/16" thickness; cut a rectangle 6" x 15¾". Measure down 1¾" from the top right-hand corner and cut in a straight line to the corner on the top left-hand side. Turn the shape around and repeat on the opposite end. You now have the angles for rolling the scroll. Roll the top and bottom edges at this angle as shown until the two long sides measure 10" in length. The two sides will not be level because of the angle of the rolled edges. The parchment can now be "aged" by making small cuts at random in the unrolled edges of the scroll with a sharp knife. Twist the edges up in places to look like tears or cracks; let it dry until a skin has formed.

Brown color should be brushed lightly down the torn edges as shown and the inscription written in with a brush using edible colorings, or piped on with icing or jelly. Place the scroll onto the cake base and add the seal made from a flattened red ball of marzipan, suitably marked with the recipient's initials. A few sugar flowers and leaves can be used to decorate the lower left-hand corner of the cake to add color and balance.

Complete the cake by making a feather from white marzipan or sugar paste. Roll out a stick 7½" long, tapered at one end. Flatten the stick along most of its length but leave the last 2" on the tapered end in a round shape. Mark the quill with a knife to give a feather effect and brush with edible colors of your choice. Display as shown.

Quantities used:
Marzipan or sugar paste	
Scroll	6½ ozs
Quill	1½ ozs
Seal	¼ oz
Buttercream	1 lb
Dressing	3¾ ozs

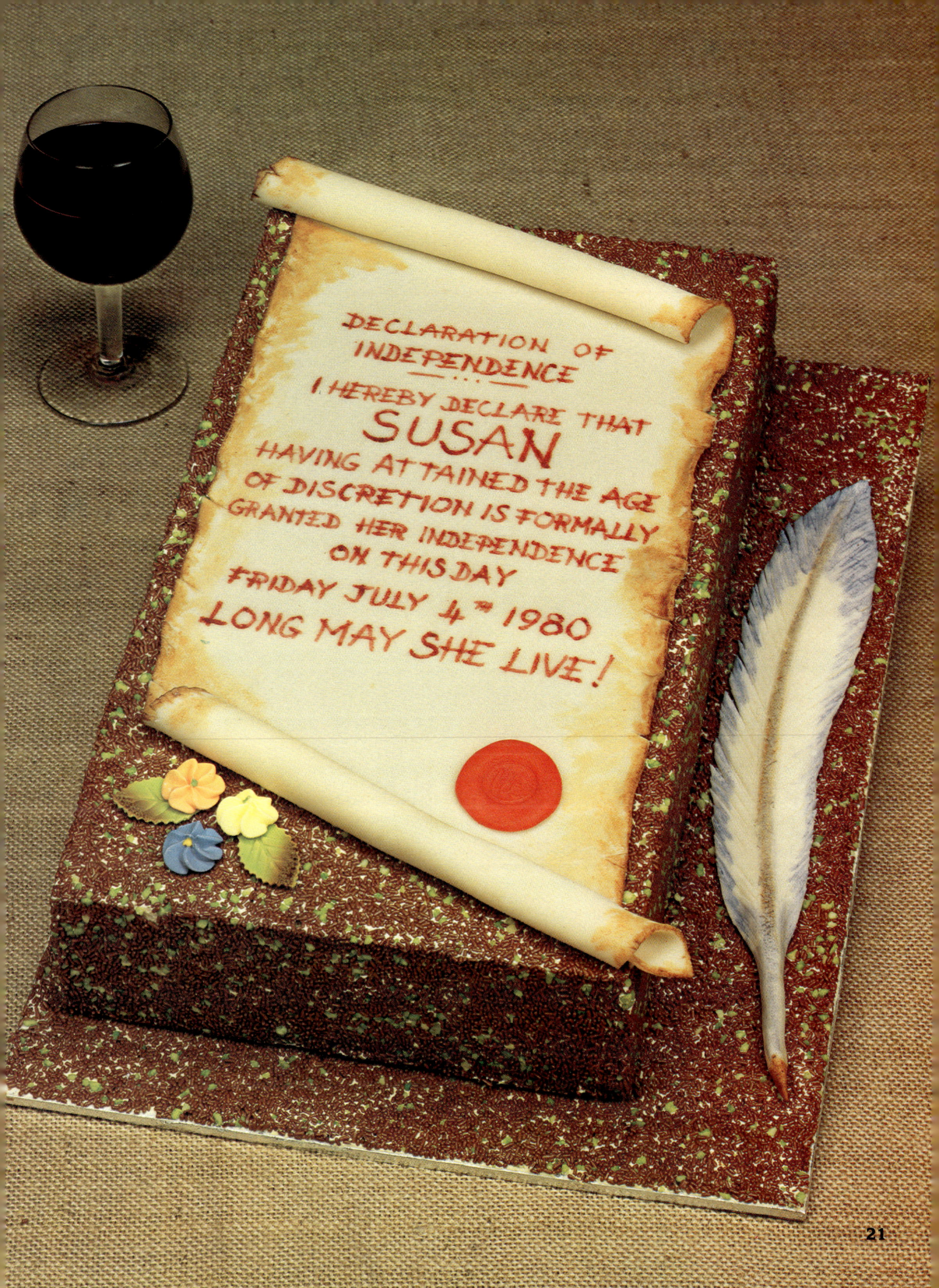

Cat

Cut two pieces of sponge or genoese cake, 12" x 7" x 1¼", into the shape shown; join with buttercream. Roll out orange marzipan or sugar paste to a ⅛" thickness and turn it over onto waxed paper. Mask the top of the cake; turn it over onto the marzipan and press down lightly to ensure adhesion. Trim away the surplus paste. Mask the side of the cake with buttercream and dress with chocolate vermicelli or lightly roasted chopped nuts.

Make the face by cutting a 4½" disc from ⅛" thick orange marzipan and place on the head section of the cake. From the same sheet cut an oval 2¼" x 1½" and after removing a small triangular piece from the bottom edge, stick into place on the disc as shown. This forms the cheeks.

Make the nose from a ball-shaped piece of chocolate marzipan which has been rolled slightly to make it oval and place in position. Make the whiskers from chocolate marzipan rolled to a thin strand 12" long and cut into six 2" pieces. Taper the ends and stick on as shown. Use green marzipan rolled to a ⅛" thickness for the eyes; cut two oval pieces 1½" x 1". Cut away ⅓ of the length from each and place on the face as illustrated. Two ¾" chocolate discs are placed on top to complete the eyes.

The ears are made from orange marzipan or sugar paste cut in triangles measuring 1¾" on all sides. Chocolate triangles are placed on top; leave a ⅛" margin of the orange part of the ear uncovered on all sides. Bend the bottom two corners to shape the ears; attach to the head. To complete the face add a red tongue and a collar from chocolate marzipan, 3½" x ½" x ⅛".

Roll out a stick of orange marzipan 7" in length and tapered to a point at one end. Place onto the cake as shown to make the tail. The paws are made from two small oval pieces of marzipan which are then marked with the back of a knife to form the toes. Place into position with one paw covering the small end of the tail.

Complete the cake by putting a bell or some other decoration on the collar and write the required inscription on the cat's tummy.

Quantities used:

Marzipan or sugar paste

Top	5½ ozs
Face	1½ ozs
Cheeks	¼ oz
Nose	¼ oz
Ears	½ oz for 2
Collar	¼ oz
Eyes (green)	¼ oz for 2
Eyes (chocolate)	¼ oz for 2
Tail	1¾ ozs
Paws	½ oz each
Whiskers	¼ oz for 6
Tongue	⅛ oz
Buttercream	12 ozs
Vermicelli	2¼ ozs

Camping

Join two pieces of genoese cake, 8" x 5" x 1¼", with buttercream. Split a third piece of the same size down its length to form two pieces 8" x 2½". Join these two smaller pieces with buttercream; place in a refrigerator or freezer until buttercream has hardened. Remove from freezer and stand upright on one end. With a sharp, warmed knife cut diagonally down its length from one edge to the other, forming two triangles. Join the two long, uncut sides with buttercream, forming one large triangle. Mask the top of the base block with buttercream, place the triangular cake on top and press down. Mask one end of the cake with buttercream and dress with chocolate vermicelli.

Roll out colored marzipan or sugar paste to a ⅛" thickness and from it cut one panel 9" x 8½" for the roof, two panels 8" x 2¾" for the sides and two pieces to fit the ends of the cake (this is best done by making a template from paper to fit the end; place it on the marzipan to get the exact shape).

Mask the sides and the back of the cake with buttercream and put the side and back panels into place. Mask the sloping top of the cake and position the roof panel so each edge has a ½" overlap. Cut the other end panel lengthwise into two pieces and roll as shown. Attach these panels to the vermicelli-dressed end of the tent with buttercream.

The cake should now be placed on a board which has been suitably dressed with a green covering, i.e., green nuts. Roll out a tent pole 5" long from brown marzipan or sugar paste and stick on to the front over the vermicelli. Pierce two small holes into the top of the tent at the ends of the cake and insert two pole tops ½" long. Before placing the ropes into position pinch the marzipan between the thumb and forefinger in the places shown along the overlapping roof panel. The ropes are made of uncooked spaghetti and are stuck into place with chocolate. The logs and camp fire are made of chocolate sticks with red and yellow marzipan for the flames.

Quantities used:

Marzipan or sugar paste

Roof	8 ozs
Sides	2 ozs each
End panels	2 ozs each
Pole and tops	¼ oz
Fire (red)	⅛ oz
Fire (yellow)	⅛ oz
Buttercream	10 ozs
Vermicelli	½ oz

Four 1' strands of spaghetti
Chocolate sticks

Draught Board (Checkers)

Join with buttercream two 9" x 9" x 1¼" squares of cake, one yellow and one chocolate. Spread a thin layer of buttercream on the top surface of the cake.

Roll out white marzipan or sugar paste ⅛" thick to cover an area 9" x 9". Turn the marzipan over onto a clean piece of waxed paper. Turn the cake over onto it so that the creamed surface sticks to the marzipan. With a sharp knife trim the marzipan to size. Carefully turn cake over onto foil covered board.

Mark in the squares on top of the cake with the back of a long knife or the edge of a ruler. Measure ½" in from the edge of the cake and make the first line by pressing down into the marzipan with the marker. Now measure off at 1" intervals across the cake and mark in the lines, finishing up with another ½" border. Turn the cake and repeat to form the squares. You should have 64 squares with a ½" border.

Roll out green marzipan or sugar paste to ⅛" thick. Cut four strips ½" wide and 10" long. Dampen the ½" borders of the cake and lay the strips onto them overlapping the corners as illustrated. Cut down through the overlaps diagonally with a sharp knife to form a mitred join. Remove the surplus marzipan to complete the border.

Mask the sides of the cake with buttercream and dress with dark chocolate vermicelli.

Roll out chocolate marzipan or sugar paste to 1/16" thick. It is important that this marzipan is very thin or it will spoil the finished effect. Cut from it strips 1" wide then cut each strip in 1" sections to form squares. You will need thirty-two squares for the completion of the board.

Dampen the top of the cake very lightly and stick the chocolate squares on alternate white squares as shown in the illustration.

Complete the cake using either chocolate and white mints or cut the draughts (checkers) from chocolate and white marzipan or sugar paste.

If any inscription is to go onto the cake this should be put on first and then the draughts arranged around it.

Quantities used:
Marzipan or sugar paste

Cake top	8 ozs
4 border strips	1½ ozs
Chocolate squares	2 ozs for 32
Buttercream	14 ozs
Vermicelli	2 ozs

Owl

Cut two genoese or sponge cakes, 12" x 7" x 1¼", to form an egg shape. Join with vanilla buttercream.

Roll out green marzipan or sugar paste ⅛" thick and large enough to cover the top of the cake. Turn it over onto waxed paper. After coating the top of the cake with a very thin layer of buttercream, turn the cake over onto it. Press down lightly to ensure adhesion and trim excess.

Coat the side of the cake with buttercream and dress with roasted chopped nuts.

Make the face by rolling two pieces of brown marzipan or sugar paste to form sticks 5½" long. Flatten them to make a ribbon ½" wide and after marking them across with a table fork bend them around a 1¼" diameter cutter or disc to form a ring. Dampen the ends and press to join. Arrange them on the cake as shown. Make a beak from yellow marzipan or sugar paste ⅛" thick and cut to form a triangle with two sides 1½" in length and the other 1¼". Place into position between the face rings, touching each one. Cover the top with a piece of brown marzipan which has been marked like face rings. From yellow marzipan cut two circles 1¾" diameter for the eyes, and place them into position. For the pupils cut two 1" diameter circles from ⅛" thick chocolate marzipan or sugar paste.

Roll brown marzipan or sugar paste ⅛" thick and mark with twin strand rolling pin. Cut out an oval,

5¾" x 3¾", and divide down the center lengthwise. Trim the straight edge to form the same line as that of the cake edge, and put into place as shown.

Make the ears from two pieces of green marzipan or sugar paste rolled to form sticks 1¾" long. Flatten them slightly, mark both ends with the fork used for the face and stick onto the head.

Each foot is made with brown marzipan or sugar paste rolled to form a pear shape 1½" long. Flatten both ends slightly. On the larger end cut three claws and make the other end as for the ears.

Cut the feathers with a pair of sharp scissors as shown; attach the feet.

The inscription can either be placed on the cake or arranged on the cake board.

Quantities used:

Marzipan or sugar paste

Cake top	7 ozs
Face rings	¾ oz for 2
Beak	⅛ oz
Eyes	¼ oz each
Eye pupils	⅛ oz for 2
Wings	1½ ozs for 2
Ears	¼ oz each
Feet	¼ oz each
Buttercream	1 lb
Nut dressing	3 ozs

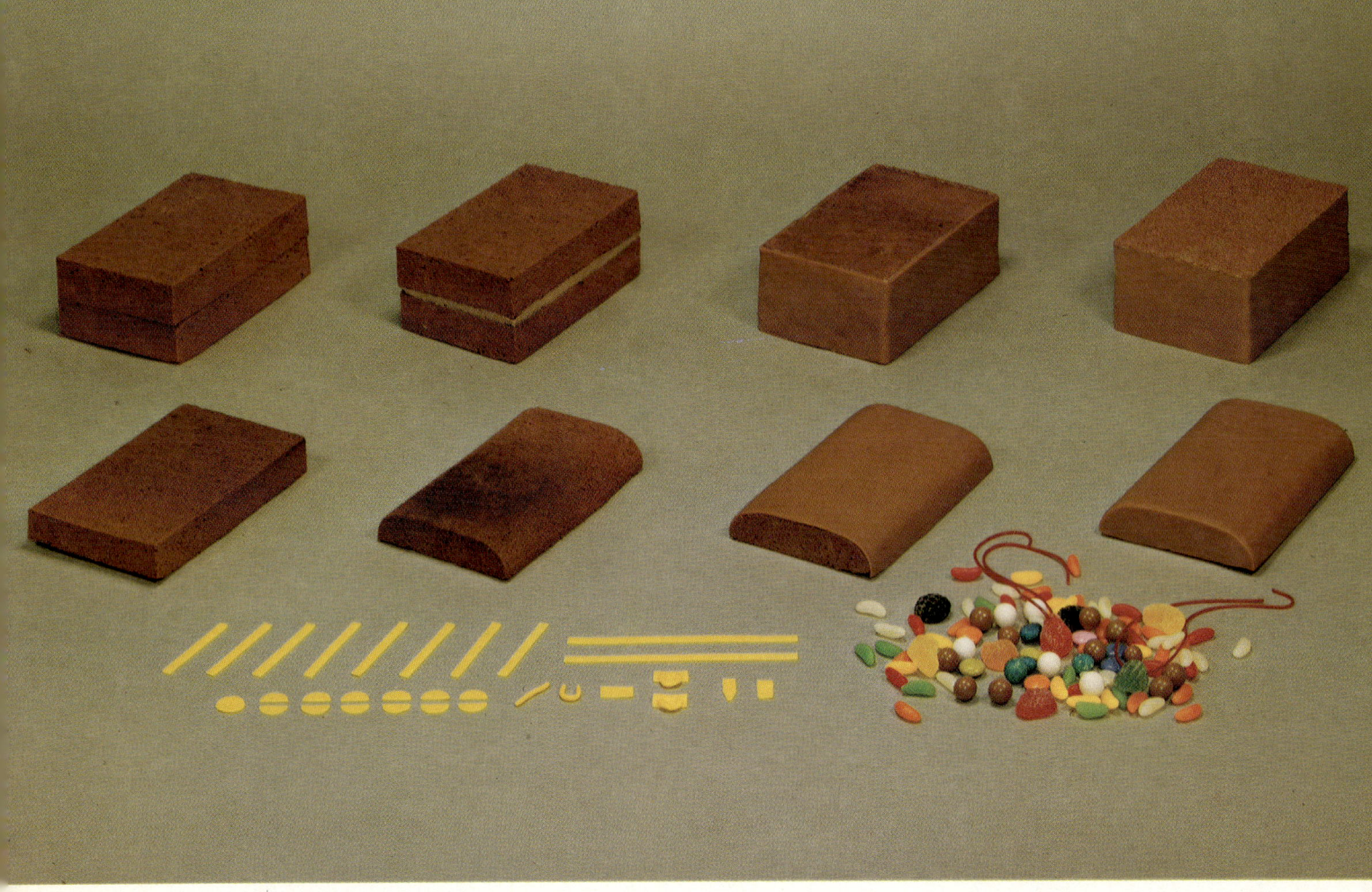

Treasure Chest

Join two pieces of genoese or plain cake, 8" x 5" x 1½", with buttercream.

Roll brown marzipan or sugar paste 26" x 3" x ⅛". Placing a strip of waxed paper on top, roll it up like a jelly roll. Thinly coat the sides of the cake with buttercream. Starting in the middle of the back of the cake, roll the marzipan around it. The waxed paper strip will prevent the roll from sticking together during handling. Trim away any excess paste.

Coat the top of the cake with buttercream and dress with chocolate vermicelli. Make the lid from genoese or plain cake, 8" x 5" x 1¼". Trim the two long edges to a rounded shape as shown. Roll brown marzipan or sugar paste ⅛" thick and turn it over onto a sheet of waxed paper. Thinly mask the top of the lid with cream and place it cream side down onto the marzipan. Trim around the edges and roll it onto the cake. Repeat for the two ends.

Cut the bindings from yellow marzipan or sugar paste ⅟₁₆" thick. Make the strips ¼" wide and long enough to be placed as shown. Make the corners from six ¾" discs cut in half. (Bindings and corners are

also placed on surfaces not shown in illustration.) Cut two handle plates 1" x ½". From the scraps make two round handles ⅛" diameter and fix to the plates as shown. Make the lock from two ¾" x ½" pieces trimmed as shown.

Candies are used as jewels. Use some hard ones to give support to the lid. Jellies are strung on raspberry licorice to make necklaces.

Place the cake on a suitably dressed board and scatter hard candies along the front and side edges. Place the lid so that it is supported along its edges with the back in contact with the rear edge of the chest. Fill in spaces with candies. An inscription may be written on the lid.

Quantities used:

Marzipan or sugar paste	
Side of chest	8 ozs
Lid	4 ozs
Bindings	1 oz for all
Buttercream	8 ozs
Vermicelli	1½ ozs

Graduation

Trim two pieces of chocolate cake, 8¾" x 6" x 1¼", to the shape shown and join with chocolate buttercream. Mask the cake on the top and sides with buttercream and dress sides with chocolate vermicelli.

Spread a very thin layer of buttercream on the top of a 9" x 9" x 1¼" chocolate cake. Roll chocolate-colored marzipan or sugar paste to a ⅛" thickness. Turn the marzipan over onto waxed paper and then place the cake on top with the creamed suface onto the marzipan. Trim the edges and turn back onto the table. Mask the sides with buttercream and dress with vermicelli; place the square diagonally onto the base and press down lightly to ensure adhesion.

Make the tassel by rolling out yellow marzipan or sugar paste to a ⅛" thickness to form a square 3" x 3". Using a sharp knife, cut 2" up from the bottom in ⅛" strips, making a fringe. Roll the strip up and with the fingertips mold the uncut portion into a bulb (see illustration).

Roll out a string 8" in length from chocolate marzipan or sugar paste and fold in half. From the same paste cut a 1" disc, and after laying the string

from the center of the cake to one of the edges, place the disc on top of the string in the center of the cake. Attach the tassel with a little chocolate or icing.

The scroll is made from white marzipan or sugar paste rolled to a ¹⁄₁₆" thickness and cut to an area 6" x 8½". It is rolled up loosely along its longest edge. Complete the scroll with a marzipan or sugar paste ribbon ½" x 12" or use real ribbon in the college colors. Mount the scroll on the cake top or on the board alongside the cake. Either way there will be enough room on the cake top for an inscription.

Quantities used:

Marzipan or sugar paste	
Cake top	6½ ozs
String	¼ oz
Button	¼ oz
Ribbon	½ oz
Scroll	3 ozs
Tassel	¾ oz
Buttercream	8 ozs
Vermicelli	3 ozs

Flying Saucer

Cut a 10" x 2" sponge or cake into two 10" x 1" rounds. Join the two rounds with buttercream. Trim the top and bottom edges so that it forms a discus or saucer shape, and coat the cake on the top and sides with buttercream.

Roll out marzipan or sugar paste ⅛" thick and after marking with twin strand rolling pin, cut a circle 13" diameter. Carefully lift the marzipan disc into position to completely cover the cake, tucking the edge of the disc under the bottom rim of the cake. With a ¼" diameter pointed wooden dowel make eight equally spaced holes around the edge of the cake so that the buttercream shows through. The exhaust valves will be fixed here later.

Make the dome by rolling out a piece of white marzipan or sugar paste ⅛' thick and mark with a single strand rolling pin or the back of a knife in a criss-cross pattern. Turn the marzipan over and gently press it into a dome-shaped 4" diameter bowl approximately 1¼" deep. Make sure there are no creases in the marzipan before trimming around the edge of the bowl. The unmarked side of the marzipan will be uppermost in the bowl and can be left to dry thoroughly in this position. If the dome is required for almost immediate use, brush a coat of melted

chocolate on the inside surface and allow to set. Apply a second coating and when set turn the dome out of the bowl.

Mount the dome onto the center of the saucer cake and fix into place by encircling the bottom edge with a ¼" diameter string of green marzipan or sugar paste 13" long. Imprint the string at close intervals with the rounded end of a wooden spoon. Make eight exhaust valves from chocolate marzipan or sugar paste by forming the pieces into small cones; pushing a pointed dowel into the large ends, attach them to the saucer rim in the location holes.

Cut the hatch and bend outwards, scraping off any adhering buttercream. Make the pilot as shown in the illustration and fix into place. The inscription and numbers should now be added in the spaces shown.

Quantities used:
Marzipan or sugar paste

Disc	14 ozs
Dome	2 ozs
String	1 oz
Exhaust valves	½ oz for 8
Pilot	¼ oz
Buttercream	12 ozs

Sail Boat

Join two pieces of genoese cake, 4½" x 12" x 1¼", with buttercream. Place in freezer for 15 minutes to set cream. Cut diagonally, join as shown. Coat completely with buttercream and dress the sides with chocolate vermicelli.

Roll yellow marzipan or sugar paste and cut a rectangle 2" x 10". Mark the planking along its length with a ruler or the back of a knife. Cut the bow at an angle and cut the stern to a curved shape as shown. Allow the hull to dry or coat the back with chocolate before placing into position. The bow and stern protrude over the edge of the cake.

Roll brown marzipan or sugar paste to form a 10" x ⅜" stick. Place into position to form the mast. Make the two booms from a 7" x ¼" stick, cut in two and placed as shown.

Make the sails by rolling white or colored marzipan or paste 3½" x 9" x ⅟₁₆". Cut diagonally and place into position. Make the flag from red marzipan or paste in a triangular shape and stick to the masthead. Add the registration letters, e.g., the recipients initials. Paint the name of the boat in edible color.

Quantities used:

Marzipan or sugar paste

Hull	2¾ ozs
Mast	½ oz
Booms	¼ oz for 2
Sails	2½ ozs for 2
Flag	⅛ oz
Buttercream	11 ozs
Dressing	2 ozs

Truck

Join two pieces of genoese or sponge cake, 12" x 7" x 1¼", with buttercream. Trim the top corners to a rounded shape.

Roll yellow marzipan or sugar paste ⅛" thick and turn it over onto waxed paper. Cut a straight edge on one side. Mask the top of the cake with a thin layer of buttercream and turn over onto marzipan, making sure that the straight edge is 2" up from the bottom of the cake. Trim away excess paste. Mask the sides of the cake with cream and dress all the creamed surfaces with a mixture of chocolate vermicelli and green colored chopped nuts.

Roll brown marzipan or sugar paste ¼" thick and from it cut a strip 8½" x 1" and two pieces ½" x 1" to make the bumper. Place the strip onto the cake to meet the dressing where it joins the yellow cab as shown. Fold the ends over the edges of the cake. Stick on the two small pieces for overriders. Make the fenders from two 2¼" x 1½" rectangles cut from a ⅛" thick sheet of yellow paste. Round off the top corners as shown. Place ¼" in from the cake edges.

Roll chocolate marzipan or paste ⅛" thick and from it cut the grill 2¾" x 2½". Mark with a knife to form panels. Stick into place exactly between the fenders. From the same paste cut two tires 2" x 1¼" and round off the bottom corners. Mark in the tire treads with the back of a knife and place as shown. Cut two 1¼" x ⅞" pieces for the mirrors, rounding off

all corners. Make the steering wheel and radiator cap from this paste using ⅞" and ½" round cutters, respectively.

Roll white marzipan or sugar paste ⅛" thick and from it cut the windshield, 5¾" x 2¾", and four ⅞" discs for the headlights. Stick the lights into place and position the windshield 1" above the grill. Mark in the lines showing the hood and stick on the mittors. Cut the men from ¹⁄₁₆" thick brown marzipan or paste using a 1½" cutter for the bodies and a ¾" cutter for the heads. Trim the bottom off the body disc, cut in the arms and stick into place. Put on the heads and the steering wheel.

Add the inscription and mount on a board.

Quantities used:

Marzipan or sugar paste

Yellow cab	5 ozs
Bumper	1½ ozs
Fenders	½ oz each
Grill	¾ oz
Tires	¾ oz for 2
Windshield	1½ ozs
Lights	¼ oz for 2
Steering wheel & radiator cap	¼ oz for 2
Buttercream	1 lb
Dressing	2½ ozs

Cannon

For the carriage, cut three rectangles of genoese or plain cake 6" x 3" x 1" and one rectangle 6" x 7" x 1". Join the three equal rectangles with buttercream to make a block 3½" high and place in the freezer. For the sides of the gun carriage, make a mark 4" from the corner along the longest side of the larger rectangle. Turn the cake around and do the same along the opposite side. Cut the cake diagonally from mark to mark, making two pieces 6" long with one end 4" and the other end 3" wide, as shown. Coat one side of each piece with buttercream. Roll brown marzipan or sugar paste ⅛" thick and turn it over onto waxed paper. Place the pieces of cake cream side down onto the marzipan and trim along all edges. Coat the sloping top of both pieces with cream and repeat.

Remove the block from the freezer and lay it on its side. Cut a wedge away to make the block 3½" at one end and 2" at the other. Cream the side surfaces and stick the carriage sides onto it. Cream the front and back and inside the top of the carriage. Dress the front and back with chocolate vermicelli.

For the barrel, roll a 8" x 2½" jelly roll in a sheet of yellow marzipan or sugar paste ⅛" thick. Trim off the surplus, and cream and dress both ends with chocolate vermicelli. Make the firing hole with a flattened ball of marzipan and the breech block at the back from a pear-shaped piece of marzipan. Fix the firing hole in place with the sharpened point of a dowel to make a deep indent in the center. Push a hole in the back of the barrel and insert the pointed end of the breech block.

Lay the barrel in place and mount on a suitably dressed board. Make four wheels from chocolate marzipan or paste ⅜" thick cut with a 1¾" round cutter. Use marzipan or large round candies for the cannon balls. An inscription may be placed on the board or the barrel.

Quantities used:

Marzipan or sugar paste

Sides	1¾ ozs each
Barrel	5½ ozs
Firing hole	¼ oz
Breech	½ oz
Cannon balls	1 oz each
Wheels	¾ oz each
Buttercream	6 ozs
Chocolate vermicelli	1½ ozs

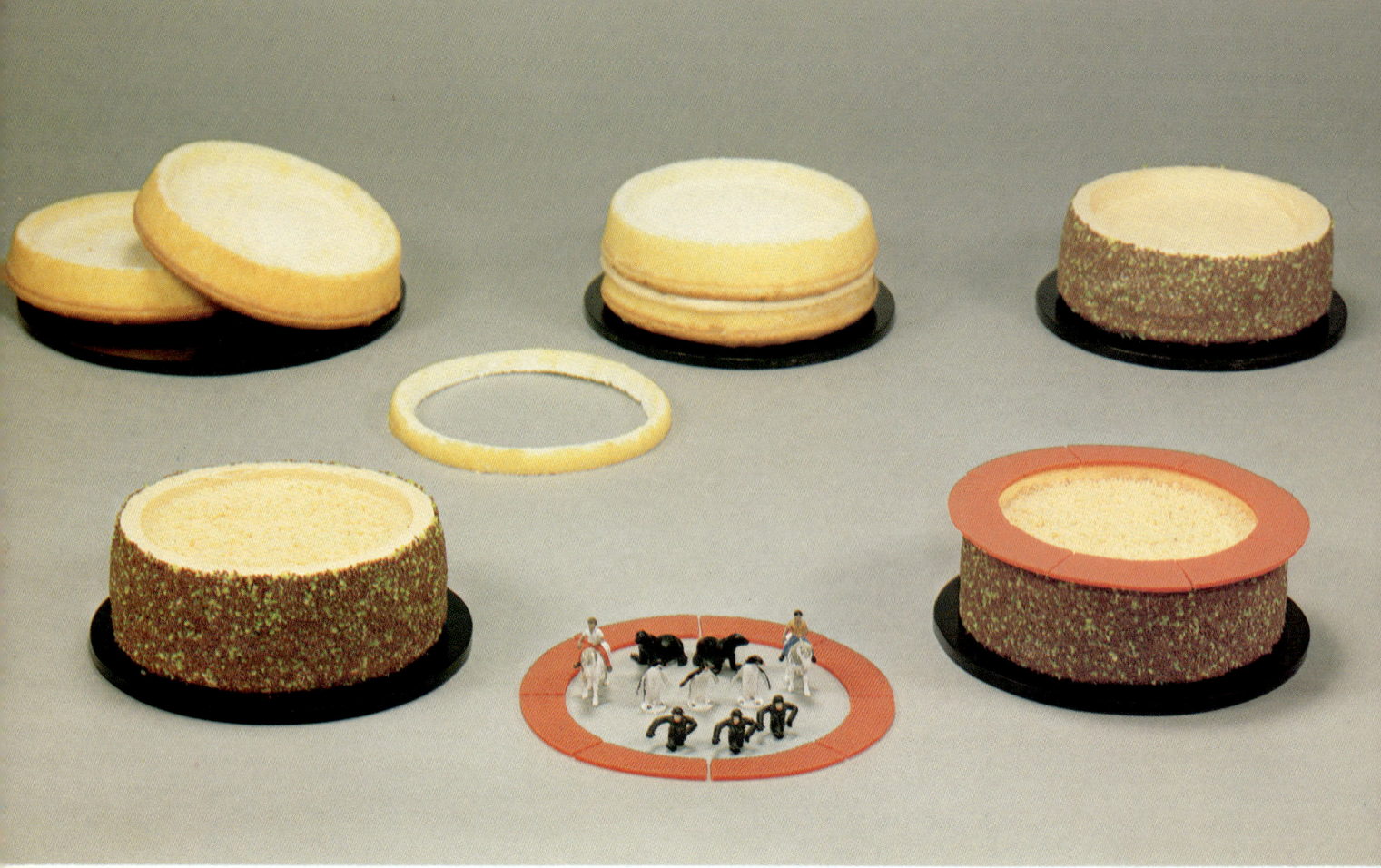

The Circus

Using two 7½" diameter sponge cakes or cake flans with a baked indent in the bottom, cut off the protruding ring from one to leave a flat cake. Join with buttercream. Mask the cake all over with buttercream and dress the sides with a mixture of green chopped nuts and chocolate vermicelli. Grind roasted nuts in a coffee grinder to a coarse powder and fill in the top of the cake for sawdust.

Roll red marzipan or sugar paste ⅛" thick and mark it with a single strand rolling pin or straight edge in a squared pattern. Cut a ring with a 9" diameter outside and a 6½" diameter inside edge and divide it into eight equal pieces. Let them dry or coat

the backs with chocolate to stiffen. Mount them around the edge of the cake on the raised ring.

Use model animals, riders, etc., as a keepsake for the child. Write the inscription on the marzipan ring. Place on a suitably dressed board or plate.

Quantities used:

Marzipan or sugar paste	
Ring top	3 ozs
Buttercream	8 ozs
Roasted nuts	1½ ozs
Dressing	2 ozs

Delivery Van

Join with buttercream three pieces of genoese or sponge cake, 8½" x 4" x 1¼", and place in freezer. Cover another piece of cake, 5½" x 3" x 1", with buttercream and mount in the center of a suitably dressed board.

Remove cake from the freezer after fifteen minutes and measure in 1¾" from the top and 2¼" down. Cut away the corner at an angle, as shown.

Roll green marzipan or sugar paste to a strip 4" wide and ⅛" thick and long enough to cover the top and two ends. Turn it over onto a strip of waxed paper. Coat the top and ends of the cake with a thin layer of cream and roll it from the back to the front in the marzipan. Trim off any excess.

Roll green paste ⅛" thick and turn onto waxed paper. Coat one side of the cake with cream and place cream side down on marzipan. Trim excess. Repeat for the other side.

Mark rear and side door panels ¼" in from the edge. Mark side windows with the back of a 3" x 2" oval cutter. Take care not to cut through the marzipan. Center the cake on the creamed block on the board.

Cut two oval panels from ⅛" thick yellow marzipan and fix into place. Roll white marzipan or paste ¹⁄₁₆" thick and cut the windshield, 3½" x 2¼", and the rear door windows, 1½" x 1¼" each. For side windows, cut a panel 5¼" x 2", measure in 3½" along opposite sides and cut through at an angle. Cut the headlights with a ¾" diameter cutter. Make the license plates 1¼" x ¼".

Make the wheels from two 1¾" diameter brown discs ½" thick cut in half. Make the hub caps from two ¾" discs of yellow paste. Fix the wheels into place under the body as shown.

Make the bumpers from a ¼" x ¼" strip of brown paste cut 4½" long for the front and two 1½" long for the back. Overriders are ¾" long. The rear lights are ¾" x ¼" strips of red marzipan. The grill is chocolate paste 1¾" x ½" with rounded ends and line marked.

Paint on the wipers, steering wheel, radiator cap, license numbers and seat with food color. An inscription may be added on the side panels or the roof.

Quantities used:

Marzipan or sugar paste	
Top and ends	6½ ozs
Sides	3½ ozs each
Panels	½ oz each
Bumpers, back & front	½ oz
Wheels	2½ ozs
Windshield	½ oz
Side windows	½ oz each
Rear windows	¼ oz for 2
Front lights	⅛ oz for 2
Rear lights	¹⁄₁₆ oz for 2
Grill	¹⁄₁₆ oz
Hub caps	¼ oz
License plates	⅛ oz for 2
Buttercream	8 ozs

Humpty Dumpty

Join two pieces of genoese cake, 8" x 5" x 1¼", with buttercream. Spread a little buttercream on one face and one edge. Roll red marzipan or sugar paste ⅛" thick and cut two rectangles, one 8" x 5" and the other 8" x the measurement of the thickness of the cake. Using a ruler or a straight edge, mark lines ½" apart along the length of each piece. Cut a small piece of flat rigid plastic or metal in a strip ½" wide with one end level and use to mark the ends of the bricks at 1" intervals, interspacing as for a brick wall.

Turn the marzipan face down on a sheet of waxed paper and turn the cake over onto it so that the creamed surfaces match the wall shape. This will attach the wall surfaces to the cake to show the brickwork. Cream the two side surfaces and the back and dress with roasted chopped nuts. Mount on a suitably dressed board.

Make Humpty by joining two pieces of genoese cake, 4" x 3" x 1¼", with buttercream. After freezing to set the cream, carve as shown to make an egg shape. (Alternatively, bake two half egg shapes from sponge or other cake and join.)

Using two 5" discs of yellow marzipan or sugar paste, ⅛" thick, cover the egg shape completely as shown. Roll yellow paste in a 14" x ½" stick. Cut two 4" lengths for the legs and two 3" lengths for the arms. Make a small bulb on one end of each of the

sticks and flatten. Cut a thumb on the flattened portion of the shorter sticks as shown and flatten the other end at right angles to the hand.

Place the legs into position on the wall and mount Humpty onto them. Fix the arms into place as shown. Add a ball of yellow marzipan for the nose. Cut the white part of the eyes from ⅛" thick white marzipan or sugar paste ¾" diameter and the dark parts from chocolate paste ⅛" thick and ⅜" diameter. Make the red mouth from a crescent cut from a 1½" disc ⅛" thick. Stick the eyes and mouth into place. An inscription may be written on the wall.

Quantities used:

Marzipan or sugar paste	
Front wall	4 ozs
Top wall	2 ozs
Egg shape	2¾ ozs
Legs	¾ oz each
Arms	½ oz each
Nose	¼ oz
Mouth	¼ oz
Eyes (white)	¼ oz for 2
Eyes (chocolate)	⅛ oz for 2
Buttercream	8 ozs
Nuts	2½ ozs

Golf

Join two pieces of sponge or genoese cake, 12" x 7" x 1¼", with buttercream. Mask the sides. Roll brown marzipan or sugar paste 38" x 2¾" x ⅛". Lay a strip of waxed paper on top and roll up like a jelly roll. This prevents the rolls from sticking together during handling. Unroll the marzipan around the cake, starting at the back. Trim away excess paste.

Make two small humps from two 1½" x ⅜" rolls of marzipan as shown in illustration and stick these at one corner of the cake. Mask the whole top, including the humps, with buttercream. Roll green marzipan ¹⁄₁₆" thick and cut a fairway of your choice (perhaps a favorite course) and a tee. Place these in position on the buttercream. Cover the rest of the surface with green nuts, finely chopped or ground. Brush away any surplus. Cut out holes for the bunkers and fill with finely crushed cookie crumbs. Stand the cake on a suitably dressed board.

Make the flags from strips of yellow marzipan or sugar paste ¾" wide cut from a ¹⁄₁₆" thick sheet. Cut through the width at an angle to form 18 triangular flags with a base of ¾". For the flag poles cut 18 2"

lengths of uncooked spaghetti and one 1" length. Dip into melted chocolate. When set, stick them to the flags. Arrange them six to the long sides and three to the short sides of the cake and number them 1 — 18. Make a tiny triangular flag for the short flag pole and stand it on the fairway at the green end. Number as you wish.

Use model trees and men (the smallest scale are best) and four tiny dragees for the golf balls (100's and 1000's). Any inscription should be placed on the board.

Quantities used:
Marzipan or sugar paste
Sides	8 ozs
Humps	½ oz for 2
Fairway & tee	1 oz
Flags	½ oz for 19
Buttercream	1 lb
Green nuts	1½ ozs

Four strands of spaghetti
Melted chocolate

Racing Car

Join two 15" x 5" pieces of genoese cake, one pink and one chocolate, with chocolate buttercream.

Round off the long sides of both cake layers. Cut a wedge off one end, tapering from 1½" on the top to nothing on the bottom. Turn the cake over so that the bottom is now the top and cut a similar wedge on the other end. The cake will have sloping, parallel ends.

Roll out red marzipan or sugar paste ⅛" thick to envelop the cake, about 15" x 14". Turn the marzipan onto a clean piece of waxed paper; roll it around the cake and mark with a knife where the marzipan forms a seam. Unroll the cake and cut off all excess marzipan.

Using chocolate buttercream, spread a thin layer over the marzipan leaving a 1½" margin on the sides that will be rolled around the ends of the cake. Roll the cake up into the marzipan and trim the ends.

Mask both ends with buttercream and dress with light chocolate vermicelli. Place the cake on a serving tray, seam side down.

Roll yellow marzipan or sugar paste ⅛" thick and mark with a single strand rolling pin or the back of a knife. Cut out a 3¼" x 2" oval. Attach to the front of the cake with a little buttercream. You now have the air intake in place.

To make wheels, use 1" thick genoese cake; cut four 3" circles and two 2½" circles. Join the larger discs in pairs with buttercream for the large wheels. Coat both sides of each wheel with buttercream and dip into light chocolate vermicelli. Repeat for the smaller unsandwiched wheels.

Roll chocolate marzipan or sugar paste ⅛" thick and mark with a twin strand rolling pin. Cut two strips 9½" x 2¼" and two strips 7¾" x 1"; cut four ¾" discs for hubcaps. Smear a thin coat of buttercream on the underside of each strip; wrap the two larger ones around the larger wheels and the two smaller ones around the small wheels. Stick the wheels into place against the side of the cake, keeping the seams underneath. Stick the hubcaps into the center of each wheel with the patterned side to the cake.

Roll white marzipan or sugar paste ⅛" thick and cut a 3" disc. Cut the disc in half; use one half for the windscreen. Re-roll the other piece and cut a 1½" disc for the number spot. (The number varies according to the occasion.) The seat hole is made with chocolate marzipan the same way as the windscreen.

Place these three pieces into position, and add the inscription, or name and age of the recipient.

Quantities used:

Marzipan or sugar paste	
Body	14 ozs
Air intake	½ oz
Tires	8 ozs for 4
Hubcaps	¼ oz for 4
Number spot, windscreen, seat hole	¼ oz each
Name and number	varies
Buttercream	14 ozs
Vermicelli	1 oz

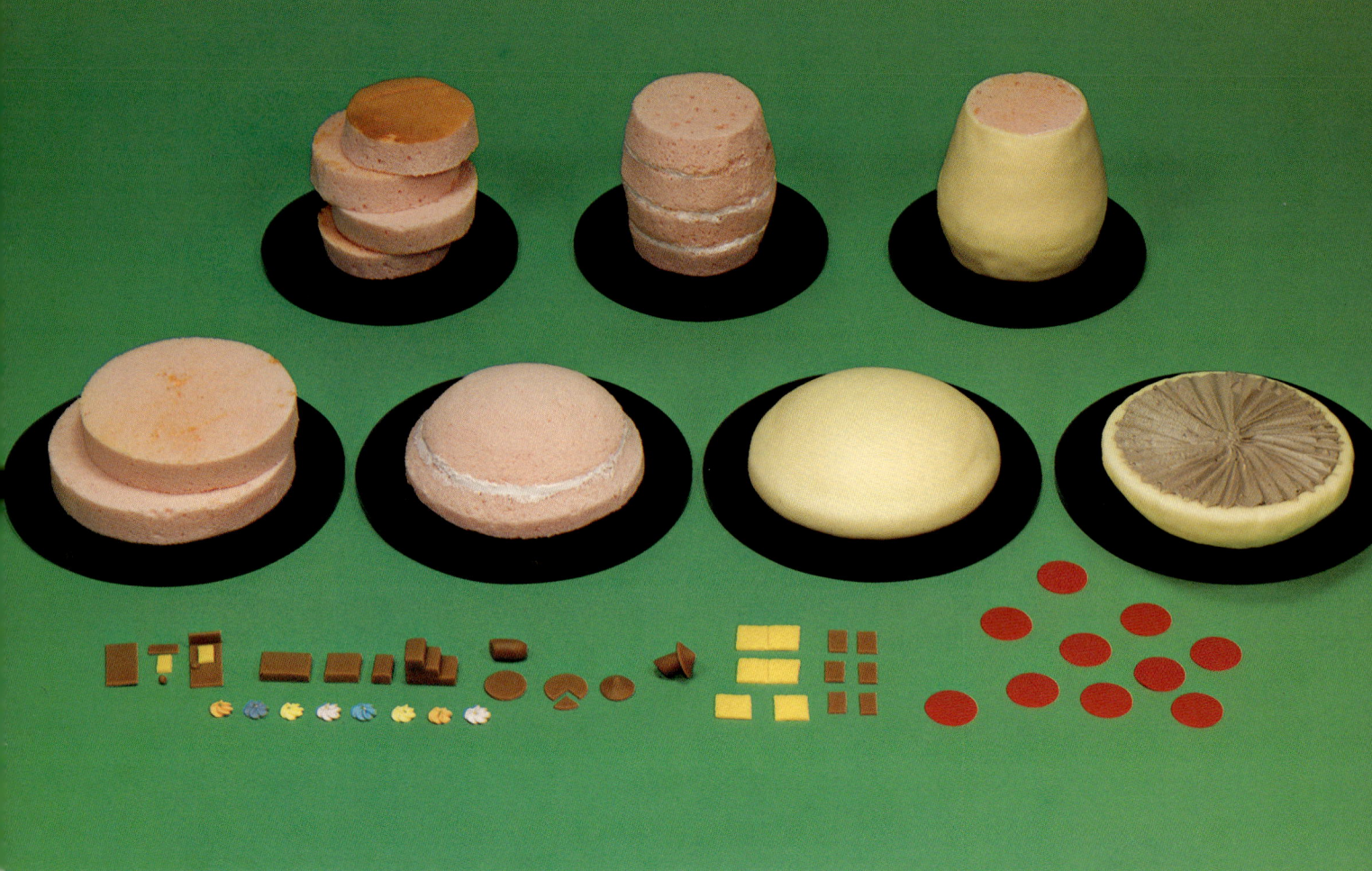

Toadstool

Make the stem of the toadstool by joining four 6" discs of sponge or genoese cake with buttercream. Each disc should be about 1¼" thick. After joining the discs it is best to put the cake in a freezer for a few minutes to harden the cream. While it is in the freezer, make the top of the toadstool by joining one 7" disc and one 8" disc of cake with buttercream. They should be the same thickness as the stem discs. Place in the freezer; remove the stem and trim it with a sharp knife to the shape shown. It should remain at 6" in diameter at its widest part but taper to 4" where it meets the top. Remove the top part of the toadstool from the freezer when firm and trim to a dome shape as illustrated.

Roll out an oblong piece of white marzipan or sugar paste to a ⅛" thickness, wide and long enough to completely cover the stem. Mask the stem with buttercream and after turning the marzipan over onto waxed paper, roll the stem up in it, trimming away any surplus paste. Cover the top by rolling out paste as for the stem but in a disc big enough to cover the dome with a ½" overlap. Mask the dome and wrap the disc over it, carefully tucking the edge underneath. Make the gills on the underside of the dome by spreading buttercream up to the edge of the marzipan and then "waving" it with the edge of a pallet knife. The top can now be placed onto the stem.

Cut out ten 1½" spots from red marzipan or sugar paste rolled to a ¹⁄₁₆" thickness. Stick into place on top of the toadstool.

Cut the windows from ⅛" thick yellow paste. You need two windows 1" x 1¼"; two 1" x 1¾" and one ½" x ¾". Mark them in a diamond pattern with a knife and stick into place, reserving the smallest one for the door. The six shutters, door and canopy are made from ⅛" thick brown paste. The door should be 1" x 2", the canopy ½" x 1", and the shutters ½" x 1¼". Cut out a very small disc for the doornob. Make the chimney from brown paste as shown, the top being cut from a 1¼" diameter cutter. The base is 1¼" long, cut at an angle to match the slope of the dome. Using brown paste ¼" thick, cut steps measuring 1" x 1½", 1" x 1" and 1" x ½". Place on top of each other as shown.

Place the finished cake on a suitably dressed board and position the steps under the door. Decorate the "garden" as required and add an inscription if desired.

Quantities used:
Marzipan or sugar paste

Stem	8 ozs
Top	9 ozs
Spots	¾ oz for 10
Steps	1 oz for 3
Door, canopy, shutters	¼ oz
Chimney	¼ oz
Windows	1 oz for 5
Buttercream	12 ozs

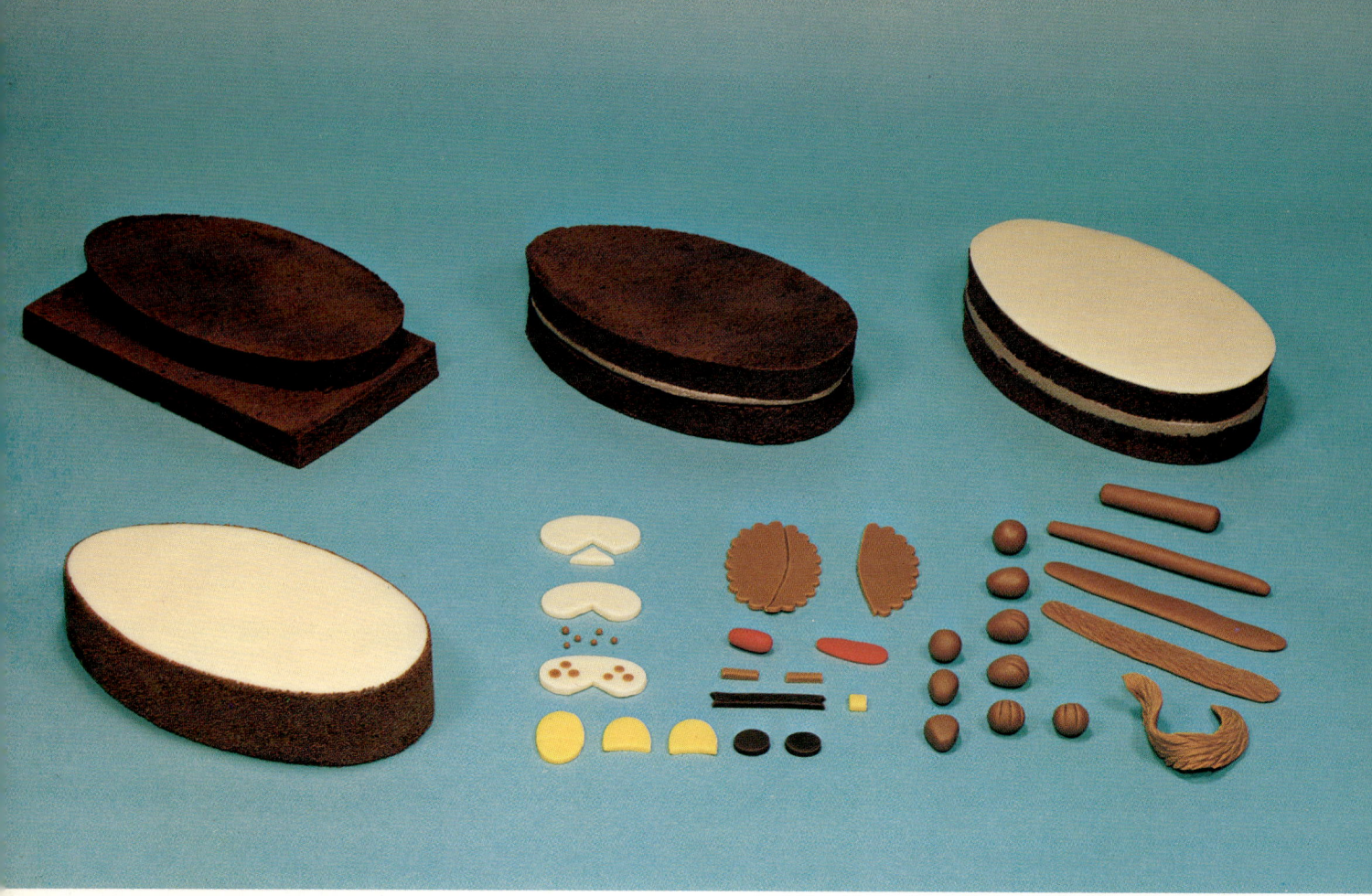

Dog

Using two pieces of chocolate cake 12" x 7" x 1¼", cut to the oval shape shown and join with buttercream. Roll out white marzipan or sugar paste ⅛" thick and turn it over onto waxed paper. Mask the top of the cake and place it onto the marzipan so that the cream sticks to it. Press down lightly and trim away the surplus paste. Mask the sides of the cake and dress with chocolate vermicelli.

Make the ears from a ⅛" thick sheet of brown marzipan or sugar paste. Cut out a fluted oval with a 5" x 3" cutter and trim to fit the edge of the cake. Repeat for the other ear and place into position. Make the cheeks from ⅛" thick white marzipan cut with a 3¼" x 2" oval cutter. Remove a small triangular piece from the bottom edge and stick into place as shown. Make six tiny balls of paste for the cheek spots, flatten them into a ¼" diameter and stick into place. The yellow eye parts are cut from ⅛" thick paste with a 2¼" x 1½" oval cutter, the bottom portion of which is cut away to fit up to the cheeks. Complete the eyes with two 1" chocolate marzipan discs ⅛" thick.

Make the nose from a ball of brown marzipan pressed to a triangular shape as illustrated; stick into place. Make the tongue from red paste and place into position curled over the cheek. Put on the collar made from chocolate marzipan or paste 3½" x ½" x ⅛" and decorate with a small square of yellow paste for the buckle. The eyebrows are cut from ⅛" thick brown paste to measure 1" x ¼" and are placed as shown.

Make the paws from balls of brown marzipan or sugar paste rolled to an oval shape. Mark in the toes with the back of a knife and stick into place. Flatten the back end of the lower paws and set them to stand out. Make the tail by rolling a stick of brown marzipan to a 7½" length and flatten it. Mark by pulling a table fork across the surface to give a hairy effect. Curl up over the paws when sticking into position.

Quantities used:

Marzipan or sugar paste

Top	7 ozs
Ears	¾ oz each
Eyes (yellow) and buckle	¾ oz
Eyes (chocolate)	¼ oz each
Cheeks	¾ oz
Nose	¼ oz
Paws	½ oz each
Tongue	¼ oz
Tail	1¼ ozs
Eyebrows	¼ oz for 2
6 spots	⅛ oz
Collar	¼ oz
Buttercream	1 lb
Vermicelli	2 ozs

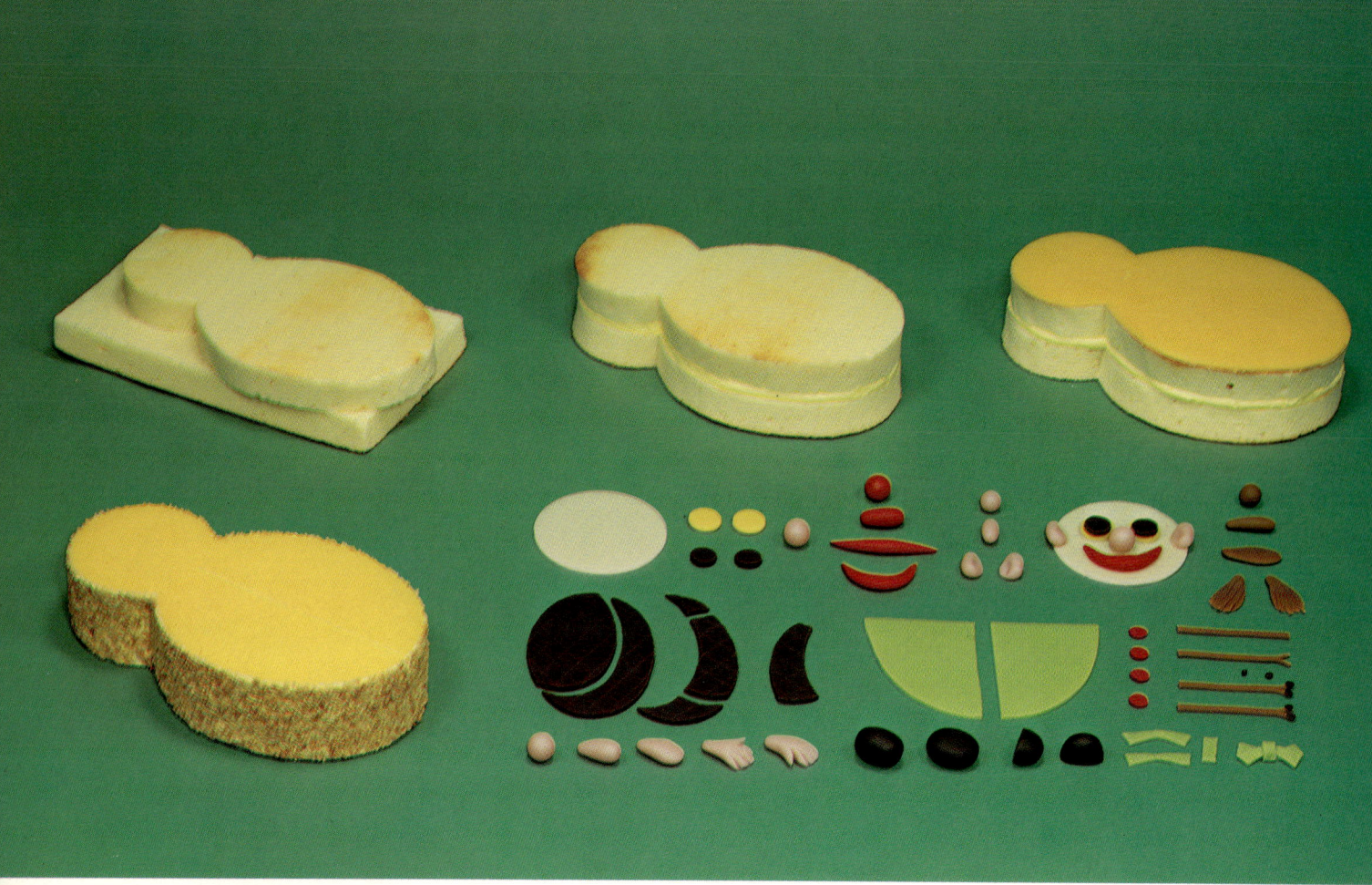

Clown

Cut the head and body as shown, from two pieces of sponge or genoese cake, 12" x 7" x 1¼"; join with buttercream. Roll out yellow marzipan or sugar paste ⅛" thick and turn onto waxed paper. Mask the top of the cake with buttercream and place the masked side down onto the marzipan. Press down lightly and trim excess. Turn the cake back onto its base. Mask the side of the cake and dress with roasted chopped nuts, then mark a line on the top of the cake from center bottom to the neck level.

Cut a 4⅜" disc from white marzipan or sugar paste ⅛" thick and place into position to form the face. Make the eyes from two yellow paste 1" discs and two chocolate paste ¾" discs. The nose is a ball of pink paste.

Make the ears from pink paste ovals pressed in on one side with the thumb to flatten. Shape the mouth from a 3½" long stick of red paste tapered at both ends. Mark down the middle with the end of a spoon or fork handle and bend to shape. Make oval shapes of brown paste for the hair and flatten and mark with the prongs of a fork.

Cut the trousers from green paste ⅛" thick. Use the same template for the trouser shape as was used to cut the cake for an exact fit. Mark the paste in a squared fashion with a single strand rolling pin. Make the arms by cutting with a 6" x 4" oval plain cutter. Use chocolate paste ⅛" thick marked in large squares with the edge of a ruler. Use pear-shaped pieces of pink paste for the hands, flattened slightly at one end.

Cut in the fingers and thumb with a knife. Cut the suspenders from brown marzipan ¹⁄₁₆" thick, in strips 3½" x ¼". Split the ends and stick two tiny buttons of chocolate paste over them. Put into place before making the bow tie from green paste as shown.

Use red paste ¹⁄₁₆" thick for the four shirt buttons. Cut with a ½" plain cutter and mark in button holes..

Make the shoes from a chocolate marzipan oval split in two across the middle. An inscription may be placed on the trousers.

Quantities used:
Marzipan or sugar paste

Top	6 ozs
Face	1½ ozs
Eyes (yellow)	¼ oz for 2
Eyes (chocolate)	⅛ oz for 2
Nose, Ears	¼ oz for each
Mouth	¼ oz
Hair	¼ oz for 2
Hands	½ oz for 2
Shoes	¾ oz for 2
Arms	1¼ oz for 2
Trousers	3 ozs
Suspenders	¼ oz for 2
Buttons	⅛ oz for 4
Bow tie	¼ oz
Buttercream	12 ozs
Dressing	3 ozs

Helicopter

Cut two pieces of genoese cake, 12" x 4½" x 1¼", to the shape shown and join with buttercream.

Roll green marzipan or sugar paste ⅛" thick and turn it over onto a sheet of waxed paper. Thinly cream one side of the cake and place it cream side down onto the marzipan. Cut around the shape. Repeat for the other side. Mask the edge of the cake with cream and dress with chocolate vermicelli. Place the cake onto a suitably dressed board or plate.

Roll white marzipan or sugar paste ⅟₁₆" thick and mark it with a single strand rolling pin or the back of a knife in a squared pattern. From it cut one piece 3" x 5" for the top edge of the cockpit and two pieces 2½" x 2½" to fit the nose shape. Stick into place. Cut six windows 1¼" x 1" and stick into place three on each side. Cut two doors 2" x 1" from ⅟₁₆" thick chocolate marzipan or sugar paste and stick into position. Roll out chocolate paste to ¼" thickness and from it cut two wheels 1¼" in diameter. Make two rear rotor blades cut from 2½" discs in cross shapes as shown. Coat the backs of the blades with melted chocolate to stiffen. When set, stick into place on the tail. Stick the wheels into place.

Pour melted chocolate onto a sheet of waxed paper and spread to ¼" thick. When set but still a little soft, cut two strips 10" x 1¼" with rounded ends for the rotor blades. Allow to harden. Do not freeze the chocolate or it will curl. Fix in a cross shape and stick into place on top of the cake.

Cut one large 1¼" disc and two small ⅜" discs from ⅛" thick green paste to make the hubcaps. Stick in place. Any inscripion may be placed on the board or written on the large rotor blades.

Quantities used:

Marzipan or sugar paste
Sides	2½ oz each side
Windows and cockpit	1½ozs
Doors	¼ oz for 2
Wheels	½ oz for 2
Rear rotor	¼ oz each
Hub caps	¼ oz for 3
Buttercream	6 ozs
Chocolate	4 ozs
Chocolate vermicelli	2 ozs

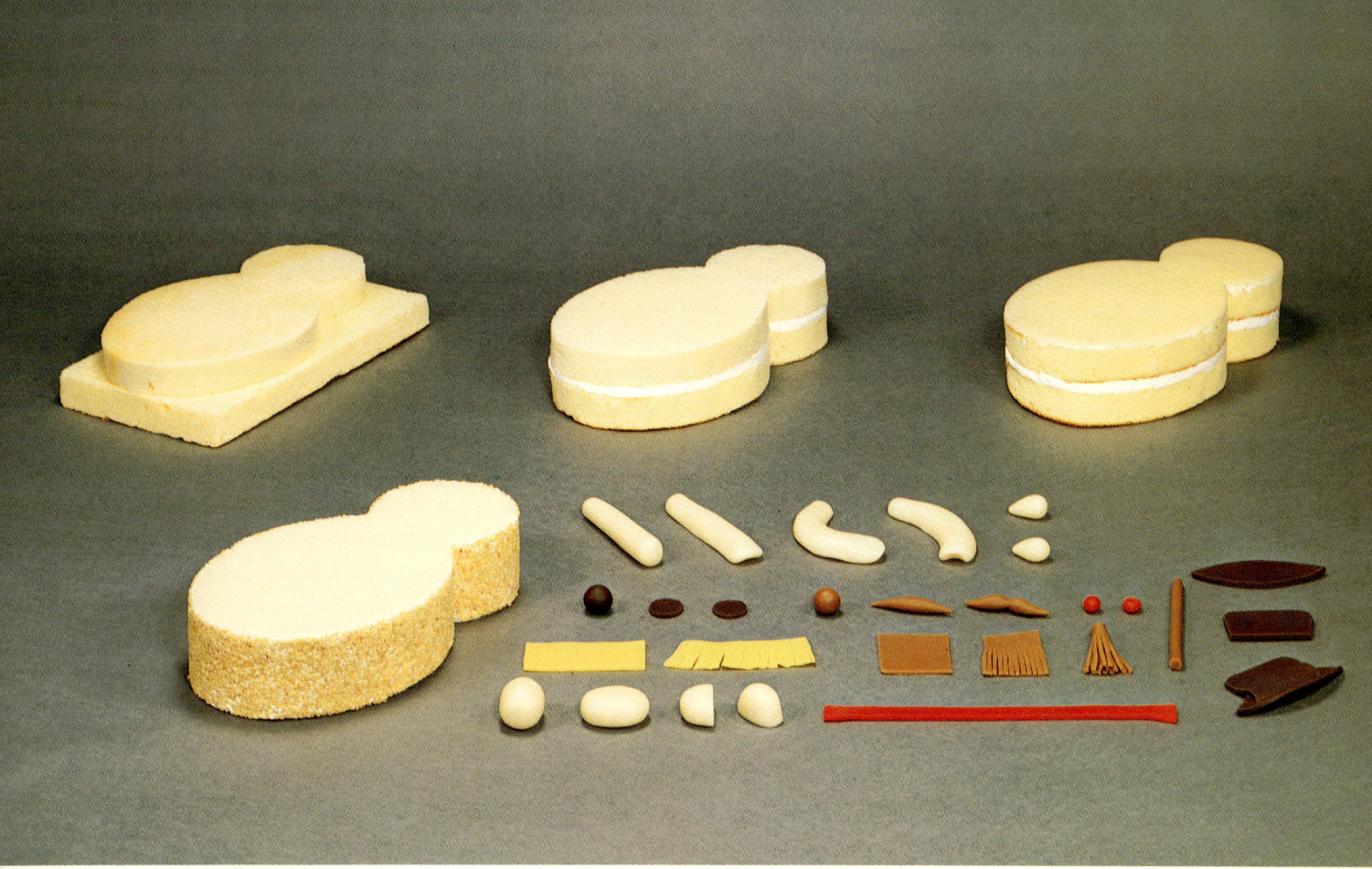

Snowman

Cut two pieces of white sponge or geonese cake, 12" x 7" and 1¼", to the shape shown and join with buttercream. Roll out white marzipan or sugar paste ⅛" thick and turn onto waxed paper.

Mask the top of the cake with a thin layer of buttercream and turn onto the marzipan; trim excess. Mask the sides of the cake with buttercream and dress with lightly roasted chopped nuts.

Using white marzipan or sugar paste, roll out a thick rope 4½" long, slightly tapered at one end. Flatten the edges with the palm of the hand and bend to form an arm as shown. Repeat for the other arm. Make two hands from white marzipan or sugar paste by rolling into balls and then into pear shapes and stick into position under the ends of the arms.

Cut two 1" discs from ⅛" thick chocolate marzipan or sugar paste and place on the face. The nose should be made from a ball of chocolate marzipan. Make the moustache from a ball of brown marzipan. Roll the ball to a torpedo shape and taper in the center as shown. Fix into place on the cake and then stick on the nose. Mark the moustache with the point of a knife to form hairs. A small ball of red marzipan pushed into position with the end of a pencil forms the mouth. The scarf is a strip of red marzipan or sugar paste measuring 10" x ¾" x ⅛". Make a loose knot, fringe the ends, cut through the center opposite from the knot and attach at the neck.

Make the hair from yellow paste 3½" x 1½" x ⅛" and cut a fringe at ⅛" intervals to within ¼" of the top along its long edge. Arrange as shown. The hat is made from chocolate marzipan in two pieces, the leaf shape 4" x 1½" and the oblong 2½" x 1½". The oblong is stuck on the leaf shape along its center line and the front brim turned up.

Make the broom by rolling brown marzipan 2¼" x 2" x ⅛", fringe as for the hair, and roll up as shown. Roll out a stick 5½" long and stick it to the bristles; attach under the hands. The feet are made from a ball of white marzipan rolled slightly to an oval and then flattened a litle. Split the piece in two and place into position.

An inscription may be written on the tummy.

Quantities used:

Marzipan or sugar paste	
Top	5½ ozs
Arms	1¾ ozs each
Hands	¼ oz each
Eyes	¼ oz for 2
Nose	¼ oz
Broom	1 oz
Scarf	1 oz
Moustache	¼ oz
Hat	1¼ oz
Hair	¾ oz
Mouth	⅛ oz
Shoes	1¼ oz for 2
Buttercream	12 ozs
Nuts	3 ozs

Well

Split an 8" x 2½" round cake and join with buttercream. Mask the top and dress with chocolate vermicelli.

Roll red marzipan or sugar paste in a strip 26" x 3" x ⅛". Use a straight edge to mark it along its length at ½" intervals, giving five lines from top to bottom. Cut a piece of flat rigid plastic or metal in a strip ½" wide with one end level and use to mark the ends of the bricks at 1" intervals, interspacing as for a brick wall.

Place a strip of waxed paper on the top of the marzipan and roll up like a jelly roll. This prevents the rolls from sticking together during handling. Mask the side of the cake with cream and roll the marzipan round it, taking out the paper as you go. Finish with a neat join and trim away excess paste.

Make the canopy from genoese cake, 11" x 5" x 1¼", cut into two 8" x 2½" rectangles and two 3" x 2½" blocks. Join the two rectangles with cream and place in the freezer. Coat the two blocks on four sides with buttercream and dress with vermicelli to make the canopy supports. Put a little cream on the base at the appropriate spots and place the supports on the cake.

Remove the rectangles from the freezer and cut lengthwise at an angle from corner to corner. Reverse them and join to form a triangular prism. Mask the ends with cream and dress with vermicelli. Mask the bottom with cream and place into position on the

supports, then mask the sloping sides.

Roll red marzipan or sugar paste ¹⁄₁₆" thick and from it cut 60 1¼" diameter discs for the tiles. Cut 11 tiles in half. Starting at the bottom edges, lay the halved tiles along the canopy, each one touching and overhanging the bottom. Lay on the next row and so on, to the ridge. Use halved tiles to fill in at the ends of every other row. Finish the ridge with full tiles bent over the top, using two halves at the ends.

Make the handle from a rolled stick of yellow marzipan or paste 3" x ⅜". Bend as shown, dry and put into place. Make the bucket from a strip of brown marzipan 5½" x 1½" x ⅛" and a disc 1⅝" diameter. Mark the planking on the strip with the back of a knife. Arrange in a circle around the base disc and stick. Coat the inside with melted chocolate to stiffen. The rope is made of licorice string. An inscription can be written on the wall or the roof.

Quantities used:

Marzipan or sugar paste	
Side wall	8 ozs
Tiles (60)	4½ ozs
Bucket side	1 oz
Bucket base	¼ oz
Handle	½ oz
Buttercream	11 ozs
Chocolate vermicelli	3 ozs
One string licorice	

Recipes

Many people have their own favorite recipes which they have used over many years, and if these give satisfactory results they will be ideal for party cakes. Prepared cake mixes can also be used.

If neither are readily available, the following recipes will be quite satisfactory.

Genoese Cake

    4 ozs white vegetable shortening
    12 ozs butter
    1 lb Caster or fine granulated sugar
    1 lb 4 ozs eggs
    1 lb 4 ozs cake flour

Beat the fats and sugar together until light. Add the eggs in six equal portions and beat in thoroughly between additions. Blend the flour through the batter until smooth. Colors and flavors should be added before the flour addition. Do not beat the mixture after adding the flour.
Bake in a moderate over, 370° F.

Sponge Cake

    10 ozs eggs
    9 ozs Caster or fine granulated sugar
    9 ozs cake flour
    1 ozs glycerine

Whip together the eggs, sugar and glycerine until light and fairly stiff. Blend the flour through the batter but do not beat, or the batter will toughen. Colors and flavors should be added before the flour addition.
Bake in a moderate oven, 360° F.

Fruit Cake

    6 ozs butter
    2 ozs white vegetable shortening
    8 ozs dark brown sugar
    10 ozs eggs
    10 ozs flour
    ¼ oz mixed spices
    2 ozs finely ground almonds
    1 lb sultanas
    1 lb currants
    6 ozs candied peel
    4 ozs glace cherries

Beat the fats, sugar and ground almonds together until light and fluffy. Beat in the eggs a little at a time. Sieve the spices and flour together and blend through the batter. Mix the fruit together and blend in.
Bake in a moderate oven, 325 - 350° F.

Party Truffles

    1 lb cake trimmings
    6 ozs Jam
    2 ozs chopped roasted nuts
    2 ozs chopped candied fruit
        (dates, pineapple, apricots etc.)

Mix the jam and cake together to form a paste. Mix in the nuts and then the chopped fruit. Divide into 1 oz portions and roll into balls or croquette shapes. Dip into melted chocolate and then into chocolate vermicelli. Dust the tops lightly with icing or powdered sugar.

Marzipan

    8 ozs finely ground almonds
    14 ozs icing or powdered sugar
    2 ozs liquid glucose
    1¾ ozs egg whites

Mix all ingredients together to a smooth paste. Color and flavor as desired.

Sugar Paste

    1 lb icing or powdered sugar
    1¼ ozs liquid glucose
    ½ oz white vegetable shortening
    1¼ oz egg whites

Mix all the ingredients together to a smooth paste. Color and flavor as desired.

Buttercream

    1 lb butter
    12 ozs icing or powdered sugar
    4 ozs (2 large) eggs

Beat the butter and sugar together until light. Beat in the eggs one at a time and continue beating till light and fluffy. Color and flavor as required.